SUDDEN DEATH

ILLUSTRATED HISTORY OF WORLD CUP FOOTBALL AS A MYSTERY THRILLER
Part Five

Arun & Maha

CricketSoccer

This paperback edition first published in 2018
CricketSoccer
www.cricketsoccer.com

Copyright ©Arun and Maha

The right of Arun and Maha to be identified as the authors of this book has been asserted by them in accordance with the Copyright, Design and Patent Acts 1988

ISBN 978-1732522640

All rights reserved. No part of this publication may be reproduced, transmitted, or stored in a retrieval system, in any form or by any means, without permission in writing from CricketSoccer

Acknowledgements

The authors would like to express their sincerest thanks to the whole team associated with CricketSoccer, namely Tim Stannard, Faisal, Vieri Capretta, Paco Polit, Javed Ikbal, Avijit Sen and others, for their continuous support.
They would like to thank Meghana of Shadow Editing Services for her excellent work with the manuscript.
Special gratitude to Uli Hesse and Kashinath Bhattacharjee for helping out with their immense knowledge.
And finally, many thanks to Tanoy Dutta for his constant faith and encouragement.

Introduction

The history of the World Cup is full of riddles and mysteries. For instance, what happened to the original trophy, the Coupe Jules Rimet? If you scour the internet, you'll read that it was stolen from the headquarters of the Brazilian FA, melted into gold bars and sold. But this is probably nonsense. Pedro Berwanger, the policeman in charge of the investigation, pointed out that the cup as such was a lot more valuable than the gold it was made of. Which is why some people think that the trophy now sits on the shelf of a ruthless collector in some secret location.

Speaking of vanished objects, where is the ball from the 1954 final? The German FA claims it's in their shiny, large museum, but this is highly doubtful. The referee, William Ling, took possession of the ball after the game and for all we know, he still had it when he emigrated to Canada where he died in 1984. Most experts suspect the ball in the museum is from the semi-final or even just a ball used for training.
Men have vanished as well. Where is Joe Gaetjens, the man who scored one of the most famous World Cup goals of all time – the USA's 1-0 against England in 1950? In July 1964, he was arrested by the secret police in his native Haiti. That's the last we heard of him.

There are also numerous less sinister mysteries. What did Materazzi really say to Zidane in 2006? What did really happen to Ronaldo ahead of the 1998 final? Or what about the Mexican wave? We associate it with the 1986 World Cup, hence the name, but there is compelling evidence it was invented in 1981 and by a single man – an American called George Henderson. It should be called the Californian wave, really.
So it was about time that someone sat down to tell the story of the World Cup through riddles and mysteries. Or rather, through a mysterious man who speaks in riddles.

Arun (Arunabha Sengupta) has already proved he is up to the task with a novel in which none other than Sherlock Holmes solves a cricket case. But now, in this book by Arun and Maha, one man's brains are not enough – it takes an entire team of football experts and lovers to solve the riddles mentioned above and help save FIFA's money to ensure the next World Cup can be staged.

It means the book works on many levels. You can read it as a thriller or as a history book – or even as a puzzle book. Can you solve the riddles before FIFA's team can? Could I? Well, that must remain a mystery.

Uli Hesse

The Line up

Herr Fassler : Chief Financial Officer of FIFA, compulsive worrier

Mike Templeton: Football Historian, nibbler nonpareil

Sonja Bjarkardóttir: Genius code breaker, short-lipped and sassy

Javier Hernandez: Interpol Agent, cucumber-calm man of the world

FIFA is in turmoil. On the eve of the 2018 World Cup, the tournament is on the verge of falling through as a crazy football fan holds the organisation at ransom. It is up to these four curious characters to save the day.

With a few days to go for World Cup 2018, FIFA CFO Herr Fassler received a text message that kicked off a curious chain of events.

The systems of the organisation have been hacked into and the entire funds for the World Cup have been transferred to untraceable accounts.

Behind this diabolical manipulation is a football-tragic.

His demands:
A game of 20 questions

- The game will be played in 5 rounds
- Each round will have 4 questions based on the past World Cups
- At the end of each round, if you get all 4 questions correct, 20% of your funds will be transferred back to your account. You will be able to proceed to the next round.
- Any wrong answer **ends** the game. However, the funds already transferred, will remain with FIFA. The rest of the money will be lost.
- Questions will be asked every 2 hours
- Time permitted to answer each question is 15 minutes
- Timer will start automatically on your laptop

- The only way to recover your money and ensure the World Cup goes on exactly as planned is to answer all my questions correctly.

A crack team has been assembled
And they have recovered 89.9% of their funds by solving 18 questions

You can read all about

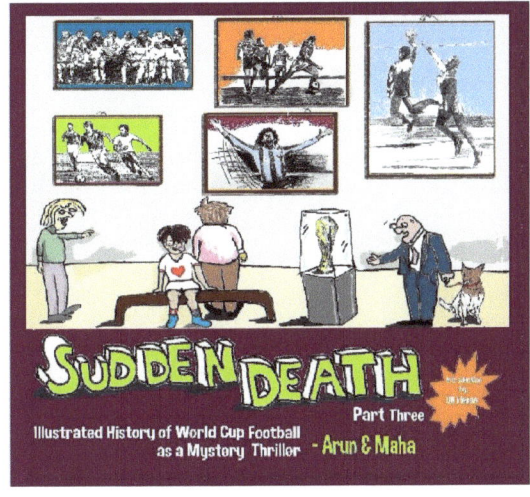 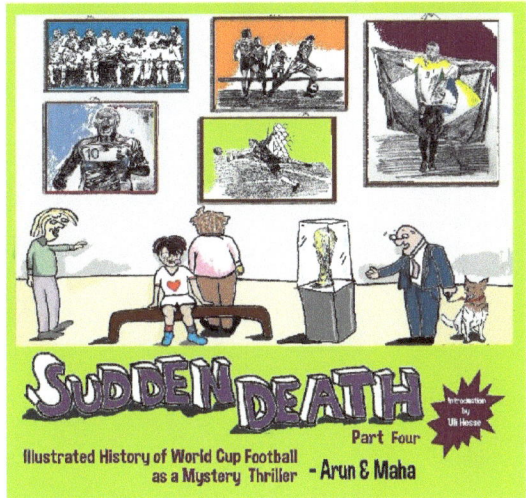

And now...

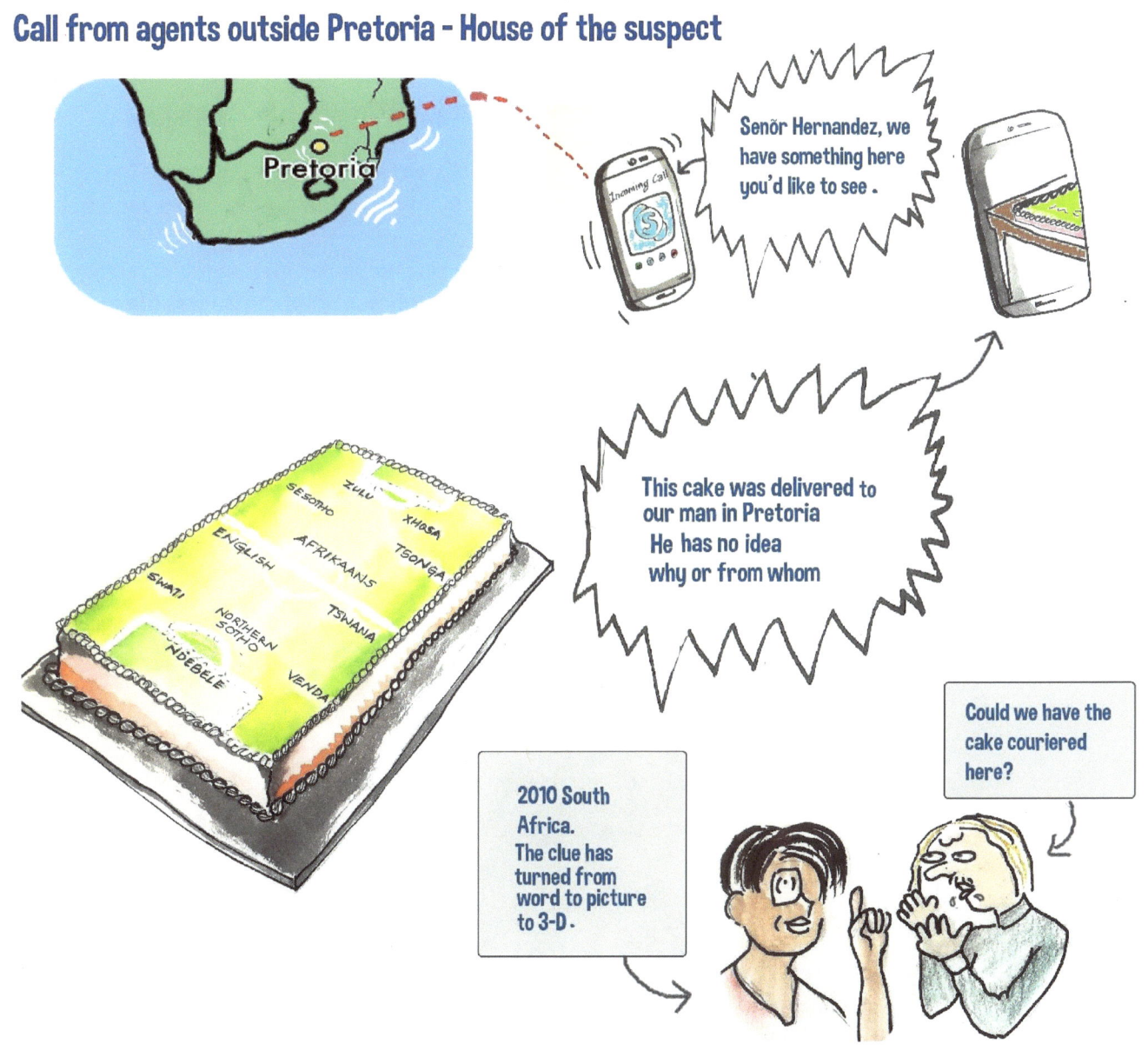

2010, South Africa

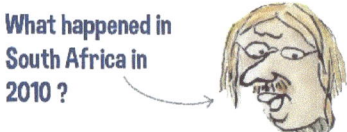

South Africa, once isolated from the sporting world, finally hosted a World Cup.

Some hailed the decision as a triumph for an entire continent, victory for social changes. The others spoke of safety issues in places like Johannesburg. The accommodation was okay, but travel and logistics could do with a lot of improvement.

There was plenty of talk about FIFA and some major South African companies making major money. But that had always been the case in most sporting events. What differentiated South Africa was the presence of middle men by the bunch.

The lead up had its share of drama. Some Egyptian fans besieged the Algerian team bus before the qualifier showdown between the two countries. The Egyptian papers said that the entire story was a fabrication.

First Round

Group 1

Team	Mexico	South Africa	France	GF	GA	Pt
Uruguay	1-0(1-0)	3-0(1-0)	0-0 (0-0)	4	0	7
Mexico		1-1(0-0)	2-0(0-0)	3	2	4
South Africa			2-1(2-0)	3	5	4
France				1	4	1

Group 2

Team	South Korea	Greece	Nigeria	GF	GA	Pt
Argentina	4-1(2-1)	2-0(0-0)	1-0 (1-0)	7	1	9
South Korea		2-0 (1-0)	2-1(1-1)	5	6	4
Greece			2-2(1-1)	2	5	3
Nigeria				3	5	1

Group 3

Team	England	Slovenia	Algeria	GF	GA	Pt
United States	1-1(1-1)	2-2(0-2)	1-0(0-0)	4	3	5
England		1-0(1-0)	0-0(0-0)	2	1	5
Slovenia			1-0(0-0)	3	3	4
Algeria				0	2	1

Group 4

Team	Ghana	Australia	Serbia	GF	GA	Pt
Germany	1-0(0-0)	4-0 (2-0)	0-1(0-1)	5	1	6
Ghana		1-1(1-1)	1-0(0-0)	2	2	4
Australia			1-2(0-0)	3	6	4
Serbia				2	3	3

Group 5

Team	Japan	Denmark	Cameroon	GF	GA	Pt
Holland	1-0(0-0)	2-0(0-0)	2-1(1-1)	5	1	9
Japan		3-1(2-0)	1-0(1-0)	4	2	6
Denmark			2-1(1-1)	3	6	3
Cameroon				2	5	0

Group 6

Team	Slovakia	New Zealand	Italy	GF	GA	Pt
Paraguay	2-0 (1-0)	0-0(0-0)	1-1(1-0)	3	1	5
Slovakia		1-1(0-0)	3-2(1-0)	4	5	4
New Zealand			1-1(1-1)	2	2	3
Italy				4	5	2

Group 7

Team	Portugal	Ivory Coast	North Koreas	GF	GA	Pt
Brazil	0-0 (0-0)	3-1(1-0)	2-1(0-0)	5	2	7
Portugal		0-0 (0-0)	7-0(1-0)	7	0	5
Ivory Coast			3-0(2-0)	4	3	4
North Korea				1	12	0

Group 6

Team	Chile	Switzerland	Honduras	GF	GA	Pt
Spain	2-1(2-0)	0-1(0-0)	2-0(1-0)	4	2	6
Chile		1-0(0-0)	1-0(0-0)	3	2	6
Switzerland			0-0(0-0)	1	1	4
Honduras				0	3	1

Highlights:

The 91-year-old Nelson Mandela missed the opening ceremony and the first match because of the death of his great-granddaughter in a car crash.

Spain, the eventual champions, were shocked in the first game by the lowly rated Swiss team.

Holland started with a degree of promise that matched the great teams they had produced earlier. Once again the country hoped that this team would finish the job.

South Africa became the first host nation to crash out in the first round. Yet, they managed to finish in front of France who managed one draw and two losses in their three group matches.

Both the finalists of the previous World Cup finished last in their groups and bowed out.

Lionel Messi dazzled on the ground, as Diego Maradona, his spiritual predecessor, stood in a suit as the coach of the Argentinians, often unable to resist himself from trapping loose balls.

Portugal played North Korea in what some hoped would be a repeat of the 1966 classic. However, the Asian side was crushed 7-0. One of the goals was by Christiano Ronaldo, who trapped the ball with the back of his neck before letting it bounce in front of him.

Second Round
Uruguay 2 (1) South Korea 1 (0)
Ghana 2 (1,1) USA 1 (0,1)
Germany 4 (2) England 1 (1)
Argentina 3 (2) Mexico 1(0)
Holland 2 (1) Slovakia 0(0)
Brazil 3 (2) Chile 0 (0)
Paraguay 0 (0,0) Japan 0 (0,0) penalties Paraguay 5 Japan 3
Spain 1 (0) Portugal 0 (0)

Highlights
The Englishmen did fight back after being 2-0 down. The lead was reduced. And then Lampard's volley hit the cross piece and dropped at a point that looked like some distance beyond the goal line. The goal was not given. Divine justice for the Hurst shot of 1966, delayed to the brink of the fiftieth anniversary? The Germans won 4-1.

Villa's mastery became slowly prominent as Spain proceeded to unfurl their tactical superiority.

Quarter-finals
Italy 2 (1) Spain 1 (0)
Brazil 3 (0) Holland 2 (0)
Bulgaria 2 (0) Germany 1 (0)
Sweden 2 (0,1) Romania 2(0,1) Tie-Breaker Sweden 5 Romania 4

The Brazilians suffered from overconfidence, and a distinct inclination for brawling, as the Dutch came from behind and won the big match.

Argentina was routed by the incredibly fast Germans. Like Ronaldinho in 2006, Messi ended as the best player in the world who represented Barcelona but did little of note for his country.

At the other end of the dramatic spectrum, Spain was progressing quietly, playing almost flawless football.

Semi-finals
Holland 3 (1) Uruguay 2 (1)
Robben was outstanding in this game, and most of the Dutch attacks had him in the thick of things. Fórlan's father had played against the Dutch in the 1974 World Cup.

Spain 1 (0) Germany 0 (0)

The Germans supposedly ran 1.2 miles more than the Spanish. However, the tiki-taka experts made 160 more passes. One can guess which method was more useful.

Third-Place Final
Germany 3 (1) Uruguay 2 (1)
For the second consecutive time Uruguay lost to Germany in the third-place play off after reaching the semi-finals.

Final
Spain 1 (0,0) Holland 0 (0,0)

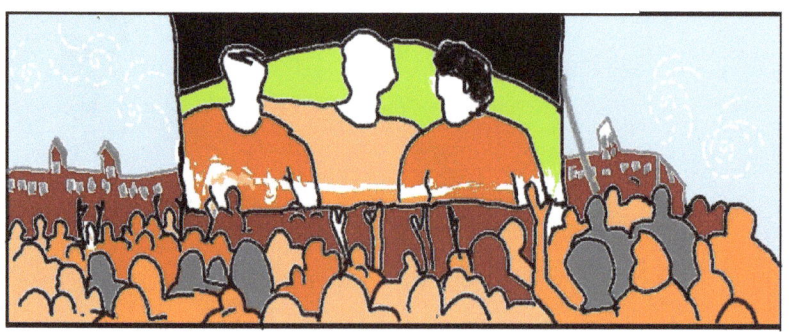

As Amsterdam became a sea of orange and giant screens were put up in Museumplein, the Dutch started the game with some extremely rough play. By the time the match had progressed into extra-time, they were a man down and pushing for the penalty shootout. However, a counter-attack even as the Holland team thought they should be given a corner, resulted in the golden goal to end it in favour of Spain.

Highlights:
Germany became the first team to win the third place twice in succession

The final was the first time that Spain and Holland had met in a European Championship or World Cup match. They had fought a 80-year-War though, in the sixteenth and seventeenth centuries.

It was the first final since 1978 between countries that had never won the World Cup before.

Top Scorer and Best Player 2010, South Africa

"I got lucky, I hit form at just the right time," was how Thomas Müller summarised his success in the 2010 World Cup.

However, it was more than just form. In fact, it was more than just the five goals. The versatile attacking all-round forward showed proficiency in scoring as well as creating goals. All this played a role in the laurels he reaped in the tournament.

Müller tied for the spot of the top scorer with the Spanish maestro David Villa, the Uruguayan ace Diego Forlán and the Dutch mid-fielder Wesley Sneijder. Yet, it was the 20-year-old German who won the Golden Boot because his three assists put him above the other three, all of whom managed one each.

Having survived an injury scare, when he fell off his bicycle at the training camp in South Tyrol, the young forward scored in the opening match of Germany. It was just his third international match and his first ever international goal.

It was during the round of 16 that Müller caught the attention of the world. His two goals and one assist went a long way in ensuring the memorable 4-1 victory over England. He scored in the third minute of the quarter-final against Argentina, in the eventual 4-0 victory. But a hand-ball in the first half earned him his second booking and thereby suspension from the semi-final against Spain.

Müller opened the scoring in the third-place playoff against Uruguay, helping Germany to a 3-2 win.

Apart from the Golden Boot, he was also named the Best Young Player of the tournament.

Regarded as one of the greatest Uruguayan footballers of all time, Diego Forlán won the Golden Ball award. Among his five goals in the tournament were three long-range shots, making him the first player to score three goals from outside the penalty box since Lothar Matthäus in 1990.

Forlán also netted the first goal in the third-place play off against Germany, from the edge of the area. It was later selected as the goal of the tournament by FIFA. He also executed the last kick in the game, a free kick which hit the bar as Germany won 3-2.

A versatile forward, Forlán was revered for his quickness, positional sense and ability to score with either foot. He was also known as a master of set-piece situations.

11 players, each an official language of South Africa.

That's the theme of the ball.

Ball?

That's all fine ... what's the answer?

The Adidas ball for the World Cup
11 colours denoting
11 players
11 official South African languages
11 South African communities

Well, you've definitely done your bit to scatter it away if it was blowing in the wind.

The Adidas ball was known as ...

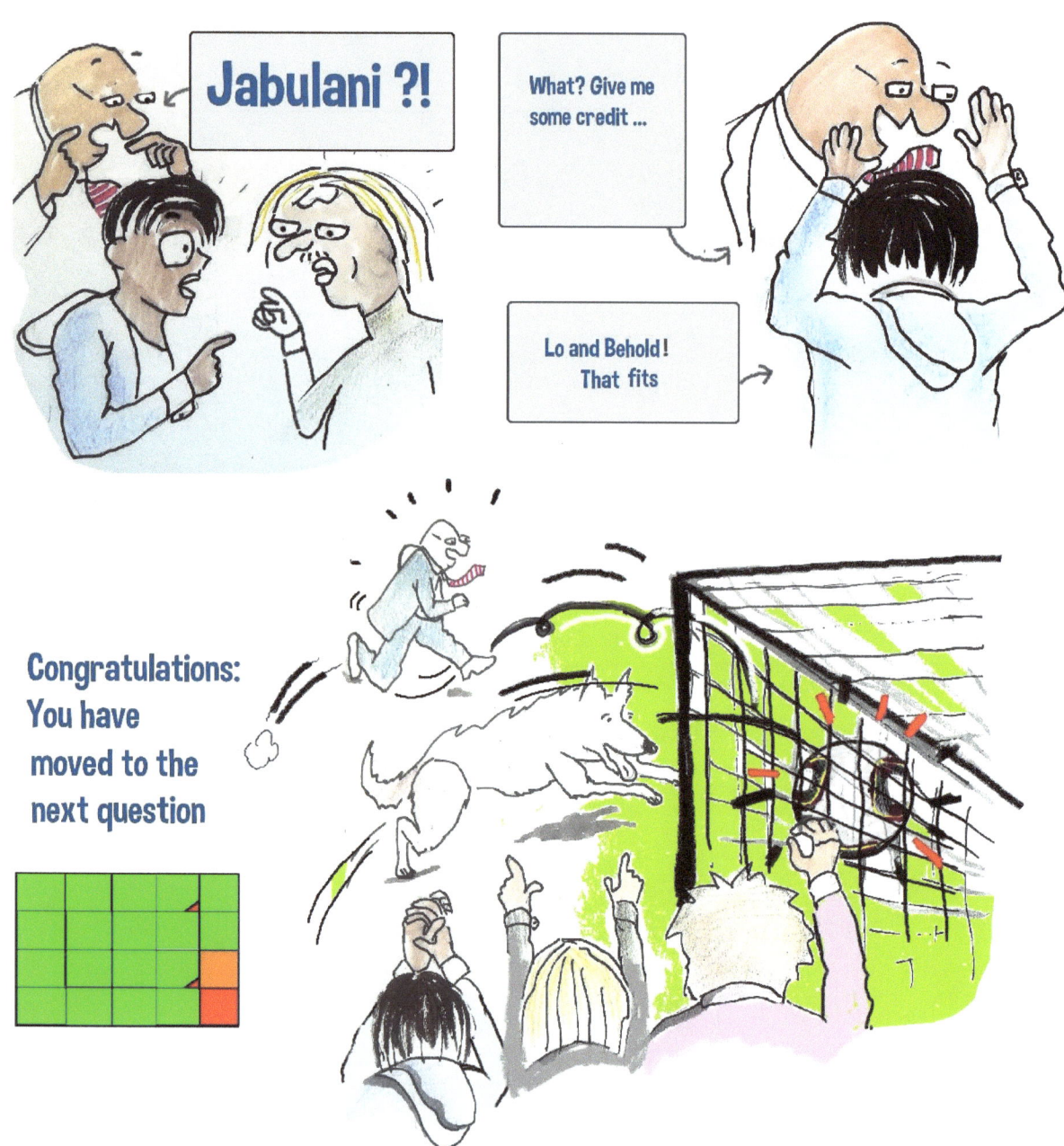

- 1934 ITALY vs USA
- 1978 AUSTRIA vs WEST GERMANY
- 1958 QUARTER FINALS
- 1966 FINAL
- 2006 GROUP B
- 1954 GERMANY vs AUSTRIA
- 1966 SEMI-FINALS AND FINALS
- 1990 AFTER QUARTER FINALS

2014, Brazil

The World Cup had its positives. It was definitely better than the last few. It was definitely won by the deserving team.

But the bane of the modern game haunted it. Too many penalty shootouts. And then there was the bite by Luuis Suarez on Giorgio Chiellini. It was blatant, and things were taken to ridiculous levels when the President of Uruguay supported him.

And then there was the obvious scandal. The controversial Teixeira was now the head of the Brazilian World Cup Organising body. Corruption was everywhere. Besides, the news of Qatar being granted the 2022 World Cup made headlines. In spite of nearly impossible playing conditions and non-existence of any footballing prowess. Some $5 million dollars spent in bribes did the trick. And names as great as Franz Beckenbauer were implicated in the nexus.

And although the favourites did triumph, there were plenty of upsets. Hosts Brazil going down 1-7 to Germany in the semi-finals has become part of folklore. Besides, defending champions Spain crashed to a 1-5 defeat in their opening match against Holland.

First Round

Group 1

Team	Mexico	Croatia	Cameroon	GF	GA	Pt
Brazil	0-0 (0-0)	3-1 (1-1)	4-1 (2-1)	7	2	7
Mexico		3-1 (0-0)	1-0 (0-0)	4	1	7
Croatia			4-0 (1-0)	6	6	3
Cameroon				1	9	0

Group 2

Team	Chile	Spain	Australia	GF	GA	Pt
Holland	2-0 (0-0)	5-1 (1-1)	3-2 (1-1)	10	3	9
Chile		2-0 (2-0)	3-1 (2-1)	5	3	6
Spain			3-0 (1-0)	4	7	3
Australia				3	9	0

Group 3

Team	Greece	Ivory Coast	Japan	GF	GA	Pt
Colombia	3-0 (1-0)	2-1 (0-0)	4-1 (1-1)	9	2	9
Greece		2-1 (1-0)	0-0 (0-0)	2	4	4
Ivory Coast			2-1 (0-1)	4	5	3
Japan				2	6	1

Group 4

Team	Uruguay	Italy	England	GF	GA	Pt
Costa Rica	3-1 (0-1)	1-0 (1-0)	0-0 (0-0)	4	1	7
Uruguay		1-0 (0-0)	2-1 (1-0)	4	4	6
Italy			2-1 (1-1)	2	3	3
England				2	4	1

Group 5

Team	Switzerland	Ecuador	Honduras	GF	GA	Pt
France	5-2 (3-0)	0-0 (0-0)	3-0 (1-0)	8	2	7
Switzerland		2-1 (0-1)	3-0 (2-0)	7	6	6
Ecuador			2-1 (1-1)	3	3	4
Honduras				1	8	0

Group 6

Team	Nigeria	Bosnia Herz	Iran	GF	GA	Pt
Argentina	3-2 (2-1)	2-1 (1-0)	1-0 (0-0)	6	3	9
Nigeria		1-0 (1-0)	0-0 (0-0)	3	3	4
Bosnia Herz			3-1 (1-0)	4	4	3
Iran				1	4	1

Group 7

Team	USA	Portugal	Ghana	GF	GA	Pt
Germany	1-0 (0-0)	4-0 (1-0)	2-2 (0-0)	7	2	7
USA		2-2 (0-1)	2-1 (1-0)	4	4	4
Portugal			2-1 (1-0)	4	7	4
Ghana				4	6	1

Group 8

Team	Algeria	Russia	South Korea	GF	GA	Pt
Belgium	2-1 (0-1)	1-0 (0-0)	1-0 (0-0)	4	1	9
Algeria		1-1 (0-1)	4-2 (3-0)	6	5	4
Russia			1-1 (0-0)	2	3	2
South Korea				3	6	1

Highlights:

The Dutch vengeance for the World Cup final of 2010 was emphatic, but yet coach Louis van Gaal had hardly any hopes of tournament success.

For the first time since 1958 England failed to win a single game. In Sweden they had managed three draws. Here they managed a single point. In the group, Italy finished third and England fourth as Costa Rica and Uruguay went through to the next round.

Germany's radical revision of youth training and coaching programmes was evident from the beginning. It was evident right from their 4-0 rout of Portugal. But their performance dropped a bit in the subsequent group matches, especially when Ghana made them look ordinary. Given that they would thrash Brazil 7-1, Germany's 1-0 win over United States was perhaps a tribute to the Klinsmann coached Americans.

Brazil won the opening match 3-1 against Croatia, but hardly looked convincing, and was helped generously by the Japanese referee Yuichi Nishimura. They relied heavily on the creativity and intelligence of Neymar.

Messi scored twice against Nigeria, which led Stephen Keshi, the coach of the African side, to observe, "He is from Jupiter, a hell of a player."

The 5-2 result of the France-Switzerland game was an exception in an otherwise low-scoring group phase.

Second Round

Brazil 1 (1,1) Chile 1 (1,1) Tie breaker Brazil 3 Chile 2
Colombia 2 (1) Uruguay 0 (0)
Holland 2 (0) Mexico 1 (1)
Costa Rica 1 (0,1) Greece 1 (0,1) Tie breaker Costa Rica 5 Greece 3
France 2 (0) Nigeria 0 (0)
Germany 2 (0,0) Algeria 1 (0,0)
Argentina 1 (0,0) Switzerland 0 (0,0)
Belgium 2 (0,0) USA 1 (0,0)

Highlights

For the first time since the introduction of the round of 16, all the group winners went through to the quarter-finals.

Five of the eight matches required extra-time, two penalty shootouts.

The Di Maria goal in the 118th minute avoided the tie-breaker in Argentina's match against Switzerland.

The goal scoring average dropped to 2.25 per game from 2.83 in the group stage.

Brazil went through because of the inspired goalkeeping of Júlio César.

The Rodriguez goal for Colombia against Uruguay was perhaps the best in the tournament.

Holland scraped through by the skin of their teeth after trailing Mexico by a goal up to the 88th minute. They scored the winner through a penalty in the fourth minute of injury time.

And the Algerians, perhaps still smarting from the West Germany-Austria disgrace of 1982, gave the Germans a hard time before succumbing 2-1.

Semi-finals
Germany 7 (5) Brazil 1 (0)

The German rhythm of attack, and the intelligence of their play, overwhelmed the Brazilians. It was their first defeat in a competitive match at home since 1975, and what a defeat!
The ineptness of the Brazilian wings was thoroughly exposed.
Luiz Felipe Scolari murmured about it being the worst day of his life.

Argentina 0 (0,0) Holland 0 (0,0) tie-breaker Argentina 4 Holland 2
The Dutch, starting so brilliantly against Spain, were a dull bunch in the semi-final. However, they would have won in the last moments had Mascherano not tackled Robben expertly.

Third-Place Final

Holland 3 (2) Brazil 0 (0)
The defeat against Germany had perhaps broken the dam. The loss to the Dutch was nowhere as humiliating, but nevertheless it was an embarrassing one.

Final

Germany 1 (0,0) Argentina 0 (0,0)
The final, the third between the two sides, was an insipid affair. It was saved the blushes of a penalty shootout through a goal in the 113th minute. More than Argentina's resistance, it underlined how poor Brazil had really been. Messi was strangely quiet, and Khedira did not play. Except for the explosive dominance of Bastian Schweinsteiger, it was an uninspired match.
However, the goal by Schurrle was a gem and deserved to win the Cup.

Highlights:

For the first time, nations of one continent won three consecutive titles. Italy in 2006, Spain in 2010 and Germany in 2014.
It was the first time that a European side had won the Cup on Latin American soil.

Top Scorer and Best Player 2014, Brazil

"For me, special talents are those who do things that are completely out of the ordinary. Diego Maradona, Lionel Messi, Luis Suárez, James Rodriguez – they do things because they have certain gifts that make them special." So saying, Uruguayan football manager Óscar Tabárez placed the Colombian midfielder James Rodriguez into a seriously elite group.

Not without reason. Known simply as James, this 23-year-old dazzled in the 2014 World Cup. Wearing the coveted No 10 jersey, he set up the first two goals and scored the third in the 3-0 win against Greece in the first outing. In the second match, against Ivory Coast, he headed in another and set up the second goal in a 2-1 victory. The final group match against Japan saw a further two assists and another goal, all this after coming in as a substitute in the second half.

In the round of 16, he volleyed in the first goal against Uruguay, and the fascinated Tabárez became a fan forever. This goal was also voted the best in the tournament by the millions visiting the FIFA website. He also netted his sides second goal in the 2-0 win.

He scored in the quarter-final as well, through a penalty kick, but Brazil's 2-1 win meant the end of the World Cup campaign for this prolific scorer.

Later the legendary Diego Maradona claimed that Rodriguez should have won the Golden Ball as well.

The man who won the Golden Ball was Maradona's spiritual successor as the Argentinian superstar, Lionel Messi.

An acknowledged great of the game, Messi's form was under scrutiny as he came into the World Cup. But as he strode out as the skipper of Argentina, the magic unfurled. A dribble past three players ended in a goal against Bosnia and Herzegovina, after he had already set up the first one. He followed it up with a 23-yard strike against Iran, and two more against Nigeria.

In the knockout stage, he remained the playmaker and created the vital moves for the progress of the side to the semi-finals.

In the final against Germany, Messi did create the play leading to a goal which was ruled off-side. However, his form wavered as the match progressed.

During the tournament, he created the most chances, made the most dribbling attacks and topped the count for both deliveries into the penalty area and sending through balls.

Although Maradona was skeptical about his choice as the winner of the Golden Ball, he had already named Messi as his successor eight years earlier. Maradona's teammate of the 1986 team, Jorge Valdano, observed: "Messi is Maradona every day."

There are several Argentinian former greats who feel that Messi has overtaken Maradona as the best player in the history of the nation.

Let us look at 1934. Italy v USA. Italy 7 USA 1.

7+1, 8 goals.

The answer to 1934 was HUGO MEISL

If we take the 8th letter we get S

S _ _ _ _ _ _ _

1978 Austria v West Germany

Scoreline 3-2

5 goals

Are we sure of this?

Sorry, forgot you can't count beyond 3.
5th letter of JORGE LUIS BORGES. **E**

<u>S</u> <u>E</u> _ _ _ _ _ _ _

   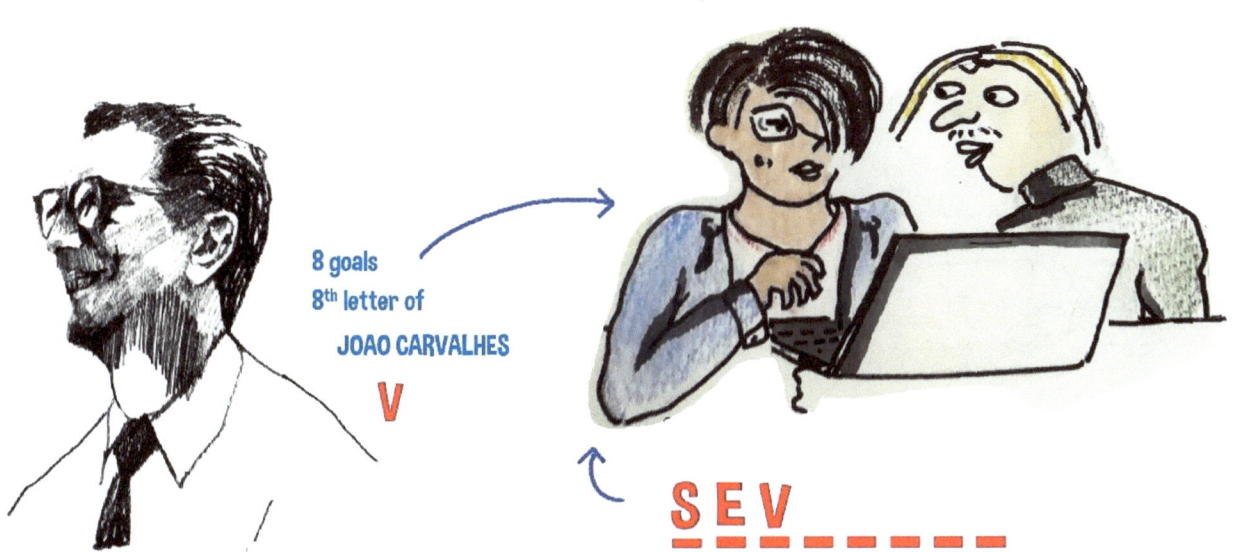

2006 Group B. I guess that means all the goals in the group (that's a nice little table I have drawn!)

10 goals !

10 goals
10th letter of GUUS HIDDINK - N

1962 - Semi finals and final
Brazil 4 Chile 2,
Czechoslovakia 3 Yugoslavia 1,
Brazil 3 Czechoslovakia 1

14 goals ... 14th letter of CARLOS DITTBORN

... So **N**

SEVEN ON

There we are ..

1990 After Quarterfinals. Which means Semi-finals, final and third place final

Argentina 1 Italy 1,
West Germany 1 England 1,
Italy 2 England 1,
West Germany 1 Argentina 0
Low scoring cup. Only 8 goals in the final rounds

8th letter of GUISEPPE MEAZZA.

E

SEVEN ONE

SEVEN ONE

Yes,
The infamous Germany-Brazil scoreline !

DING !

You've done well. You've recovered 99.9% of your funds. Now enjoy the game. It was a pleasure playing with you. And FIFA owes you bigtime for saving their ****

Mission Sudden Death. Recovery complete.
Break in and capture suspect in East London.

Also available in one complete volume ...

A Product of the Blinders Team

www.ingramcontent.com/pod-product-compliance
Lightning Source LLC
LaVergne TN
LVHW072117070426
835510LV00003B/103